HEALTH FOOD COOKING

Vegetables & Salads

Contents

D1742817

Introduction

The 'health food' approach to vegetables can be summed up very easily: they should be grown as naturally as possible, used as fresh as possible and prepared in a way which preserves the maximum nutritional goodness. Vegetables no longer play the supporting role they had in that long-running domestic comedy 'Meat and Two Veg'. Instead they can become the centre of a meal – their colour, texture and flavour all used and appreciated to the full.

If you are not in a position to grow your own, you may find shops near you, or farms or market gardens, selling organically-grown vegetables. These are sometimes more expensive than artificially fertilized produce, but the full flavour of organic vegetables and their nutritional goodness make them a good buy.

From early spring on, snap up all the 'seasonal specials' in prime condition. Do not buy cheap vegetables if they are obviously over the hill, and resist imported or hothouse exotica if the prices are outrageous. For the winter you can buy unwashed root vegetables from farm shops by the sack, bury them in trays of dry sand, and keep in a cool, dark place – this will cut your winter vegetable bills enormously. If you have a freezer or enjoy bottling and preserving, you can economize further, but here we will concentrate on fresh vegetables.

It is good to eat vegetables raw, both winter and summer, on a regular basis, since no food value is lost in the preparation, and your digestive tract will be stimulated by the process of absorbing the food. Do not limit yourself to the ordinary lettuce/tomato/cucumber range of vegetables – consider the possibility of salads using carrots, parsnips, courgettes, beansprouts, cold cooked pulses, nuts, seeds, grains or fresh and dried fruit.

Cooking techniques

When cooking vegetables, try to preserve their minerals, vitamins and enzymes as completely as you can. This means you should cook them as little as possible and preserve the cooking juices. The following five methods are best.

Steaming
No goodness escapes into the air and little food content is leached away in the cooking water. This is also a very rapid form of cooking and good for slimmers.

3

Introduction

Stir-frying (Chinese style) in a wok
Just a few minutes frying at a high temperature in a minimal amount of vegetable oil seals in the flavour. If vegetables are finely sliced, they will be ready in minutes.

Casseroling
If vegetables gently bubble in their own juices in a slow oven, no goodness is lost, and the flavour is enhanced.

Baking
This is better than roasting since no cooking fats are needed.

Sautéing followed by gentle simmering well-covered
This is the basic techique of much Indian vegetarian cookery: the vegetables form their own sauce. All the goodness and flavour is held in.

The following methods of cooking vegetables are less desirable.

Boiling
So often this is overdone and the vegetables collapse to a tasteless, sodden mass. Many natural enzymes are destroyed and much of the goodness in the vegetables goes down the drain with the cooking water.

Roasting
This method makes very tasty vegetable dishes, but the food will absorb the cooking fats or oils so weight-watchers, or those whose diet is high in animal fats, should use roast vegetables sparingly.

Frying
One of the most fattening methods of preparing vegetables. If the temperature of the oil is initially high, less oil is absorbed.

Utensils

Apart from the usual kitchen equipment, here are a few invaluable utensils.

Chinese vegetable chopper
This looks like a butcher's cleaver but the blade is much finer. Once you are used to handling it (the blade should be swung down towards you with a motion like closing an old-fashioned paper guillotine) you can chop anything from delicate herbs to large, tough swedes. Flame dry and oil as for the wok (p 4) since it is not stainless steel.

Vegetable steamer
This is a large pot with inner perforated compartments for the vegetables and a tight-fitting lid. If you cannot afford one, you can balance a small metal colander on an upturned bowl inside a large saucepan and seal the saucepan lid very tightly – with a strip of dough if necessary.

Pressure cooker
This is very useful for cutting down the cooking time of pulses and lentils. They should still be pre-soaked overnight. Take care that the sloughed-off skins do not block the air release vent. Most fresh vegetables cook so rapidly that it is scarcely worth risking over-cooking them in a pressure cooker.

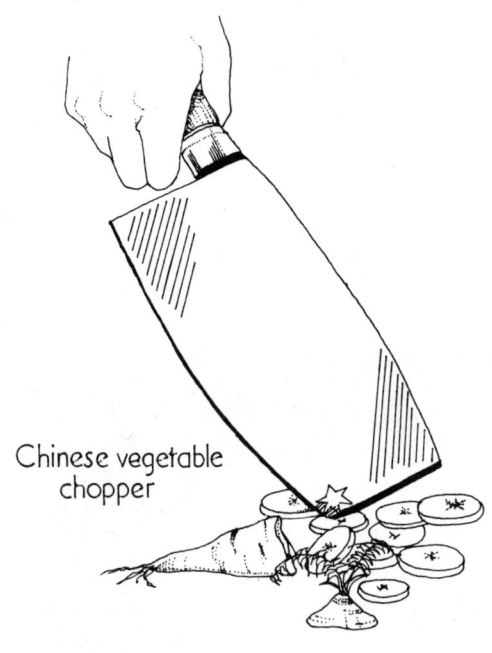

Chinese vegetable
chopper

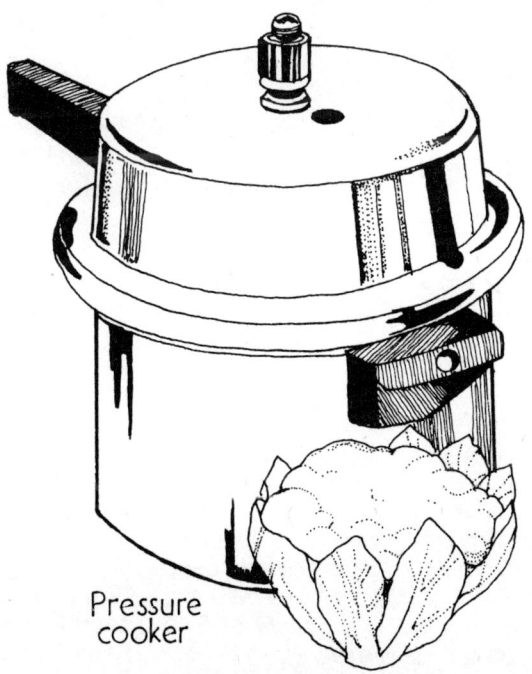

Pressure
cooker

Introduction

Chinese wok

Chinese wok

This is a cast-iron, saucer-shaped frying pan with a handle, a lid and a metal ring-stand to balance it on your cooker. They come in various sizes. A similar Indian utensil, a tava, has no ring or lid and has two loop handles. These are just as good and are found in many Asian grocery shops. Because the wok is not stainless steel you should maintain it carefully.

When you purchase a new wok, wash off any preservative coating in hot soapy water, then heat the wok. Throw in a handful of salt and rub it into the hot inner surface with a pad of brown paper. After each use, wash in soapy water but use no abrasive scrubbers. Now dry it over a gentle flame, and rub a little vegetable oil over the inner surface. This need not be washed off before using it again.

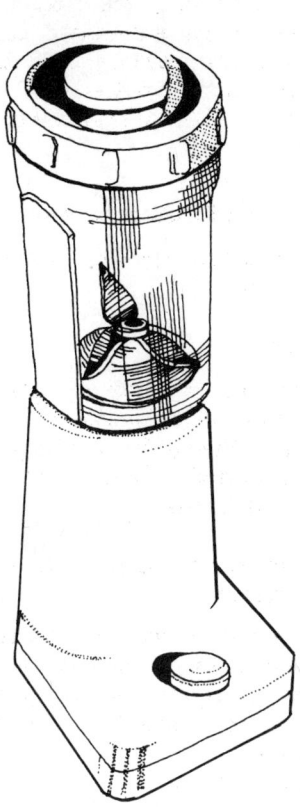

Large glass sweet jar
When turned on its side, with a piece of muslin secured over the neck with a rubber band, this is the ideal container in which to grow sprouts from moong beans, soya beans, wheat or alfalfa.

Food blender
Either a manual or electric version can be very handy for creating soups, purées, pâtés and baby food from vegetables.

Vegetable knives
Use small good quality knives for fine work and peeling.

Chopping board
Give yourself room to work with a large solid board.

Cooked vegetables

Steaming

Root vegetables

Scrub rather than peel all root vegetables unless they are very old and tough. Just cut out any coarse or discoloured patches. Now slice the vegetables quite finely into attractive shapes, sprinkle on a little salt, and place in the steamer compartments above the boiling water. Seal up and cook for 12 to 15 minutes. They will still be crisp and full of flavour, but they are now ready to eat.

Leafy vegetables

These should be washed and trimmed. Cabbage or spinach can be shredded, cauliflower or broccoli can be divided into small pieces. They will be ready in about 7 minutes.

Gourd vegetables

Marrows, courgettes and pumpkins have a high water content and are particularly good when steamed since they do not collapse as they would if boiled. This should take 5 to 7 minutes.

Steamed cauliflower or broccoli

1 large head of cauliflower, or broccoli, in flowerettes
1 tsp salt, ½ tsp white pepper, freshly ground
1 dsp roasted sesame seeds

Put the cauliflower or broccoli with the stems pointing up, in the top compartment of a steamer over boiling water and cover tightly. Cook for 7 minutes, then open. Once excess moisture is drained, place in a serving dish, season with salt and pepper and sprinkle with sesame seeds. These should still be good and crisp.

Steamed Brussels sprouts

2lb Brussels sprouts, cleaned and trimmed
salt
butter

Place the trimmed sprouts in the steamer over boiling water and cover tightly. Steam for 7 minutes, then remove, drain, sprinkle with salt and dot with butter.

Steamed pumpkin, marrow or courgette

2lb pumpkin, marrow or courgette, cubed (the pumpkin must be peeled and its seeds removed, but the marrow or courgette can be chopped whole)
butter, salt and white pepper or nutmeg for seasoning

These gourd vegetables will remain nice and firm if steamed. Once the water is boiling, cover tightly and steam for 7 minutes. Serve with butter and seasonings.

Steamed white cabbage

2lb white cabbage, shredded
1 heaped tsp caraway seeds, dry roasted
1 tsp tamari

Place the prepared cabbage in the steamer over boiling water, seal and cook for 7 minutes, then remove and drain off any excess moisture. Stir through the caraway seeds and tamari and serve.

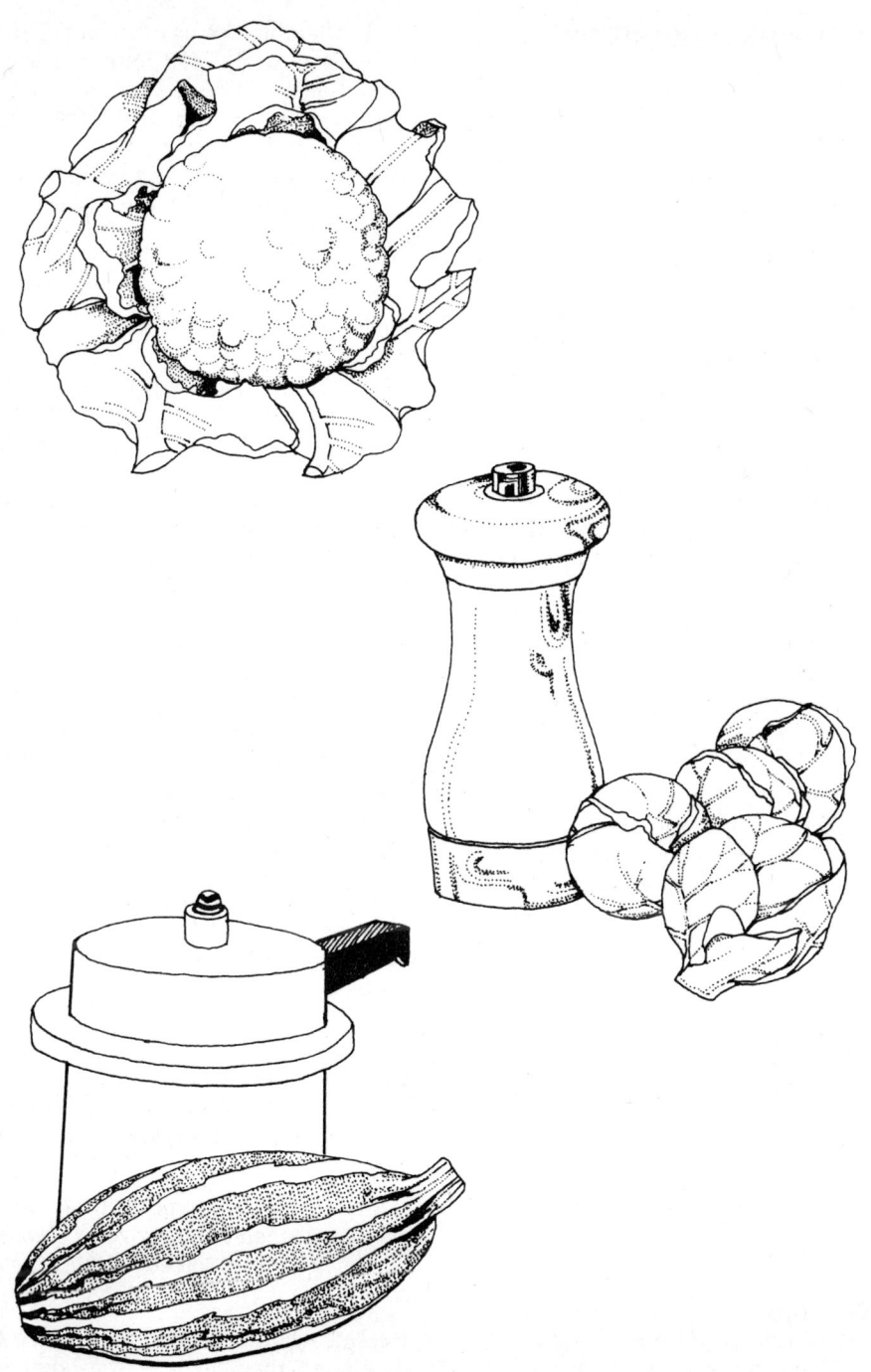

Cooked vegetables

Steamed spinach

2lb spinach, washed and shredded
1oz butter or margarine
juice of one small lemon
1 tsp tamari (soya sauce)

Once the water in the steamer is boiling, seal up the spinach in the top compartment. After 7 minutes, turn off the heat and open. Place the spinach in a colander to allow any excess moisture to drain away, then put in a serving dish, dot with butter and sprinkle over lemon and tamari.

Steamed new potatoes

2lb small new potatoes, scrubbed
1 heaped tbsp butter
1 tsp caraway seeds
salt and black pepper to taste

All the potatoes must be of a uniform size — if any are large, chop them up. Steam for 15 minutes from boiling point. Meanwhile, gently melt the butter over a low heat and fry the caraway seeds, salt and pepper in the butter. When serving the potatoes, pour over the caraway butter just before you bring them to the table. If you do not have any caraway seeds, you could substitute one tsp of thyme or marjoram.

Steamed potatoes with yoghurt sauce

2lb small new potatoes
salt to taste
2 tsp chopped parsley, mint or chives
½pt plain yoghurt
a little milk if the yoghurt is quite thick

Steam the potatoes as in the previous recipe and while they are cooking beat the salt and herbs into the yoghurt, thinning it with milk if necessary. Put the potatoes in a serving dish and pour over the seasoned yoghurt. (These could be served cold.)

Steamed brassicus with vinaigrette sauce

Prepare your favourite — cauliflower, purple sprouting broccoli or calabrese (purple cauliflower) by steaming in the normal manner. Keep covered and warm.

Now prepare a dressing of good vegetable oil with either lemon juice or wine vinegar, seasoned with salt, white pepper and crushed garlic. Pour over the vegetable and serve hot or cold.

Poor man's asparagus (Broccoli spears in tahini sauce)

Clean and trim a bunch of purple sprouting broccoli. Leave the florets on the tender top stalks, cutting away the lower stalks where they become coarser. Steam.

Prepare tahini sauce described for globe artichoke and eat the broccoli spears with your fingers, dipped in the tahini sauce.

Steamed, diced winter root vegetables in butter sauce

If your family reject swedes, turnips and parsnips out of hand, try this one.

½lb each carrot, swede, turnip and parsnip cleaned but not peeled unless necessary, and diced into small cubes.

Put into a large steamer, and cook for 7 minutes, then check — they should be crisp but tender enough to be palatable. Continue longer if necessary, since the age of the vegetable affects cooking time.

For children, serve with herbal butter, but adults might prefer garlic.

(Melt butter over a gentle heat and toss in your chosen seasoning. Cook 2 minutes, keeping the temperature low so the butter is not browned).

Stir-fried

Use a wok, and ensure that all the vegetables are very finely chopped so that they cook in minutes. Root vegetables could be coarsely grated or very finely diced.

Stir-fried mushrooms

1 dsp vegetable oil
4 cloves garlic, peeled and crushed
1lb good quality mushrooms
8oz cooking apple
tamari to taste

Heat the oil and fry the garlic till translucent. Wash and slice the mushrooms and peel, core and slice the apple. Add to the pan and begin stirring and frying. When you are sure you have enough oil, lower the heat, cover and simmer for 4 minutes. Then add tamari and serve at once. (If you leave them standing they will shrink.)

Cooked vegetables

Stir-fried onion rings (a useful garnish for grain dishes)

1 dsp vegetable oil
8oz large onions, chopped in fine rings
1 large pinch ginger powder or finely chopped root ginger
salt or tamari to taste

Heat the oil in the wok and when very hot, toss in the onion rings. Sprinkle over the ginger and stir them gently till they are tender and golden, about 10 minutes. If they show signs of going brown, lower the heat. Add salt or tamari and serve.

Diced carrot and parsnip (or swede)

1 tbsp vegetable oil
1lb each of carrot and parsnip (or swede) diced very small
1 tsp gomasio (sesame seed salt)

Heat the oil in the wok and put in the diced vegetables. Sauté for 10 minutes, stirring all the time, and if they are still too crisp, allow them to go on a little longer. (The age of the vegetables would cause the timing to vary from spring through winter.) Remove with a slotted spoon to be sure that any excess oil drains off. Sprinkle gomasio over the vegetables and serve.

Potato rings

1 tbsp oil for frying
1 tsp salt and 1 tsp coriander or nutmeg

2lb large potatoes, scrubbed and sliced in thin rings
2 tbsp water

Heat the oil in the wok, stir in the coriander or nutmeg, then put in the potato rings and sauté for 15 minutes, stirring all the time. If you sliced them thinly, they should be golden and well cooked, but if not, put in the hot water, cover with a lid, and allow them to simmer till just tender.

Stir-fried grated beetroot

1 tbsp vegetable oil
2lb raw beetroot, scrubbed and coarsely grated
1 tsp tamari and 1 tsp gomasio

In terms of fuel and time, this is the most economical way to cook beetroot. Heat the oil in the wok, stir in the grated beetroot and cook for 15 minutes, stirring constantly. Sprinkle with tamari and gomasio and serve hot.

Baked

In terms of cooking economy, oven-baked vegetables make a good side dish for oven-baked main courses such as pies, casseroles and crumbles, since you use no extra fuel. Space is important, for the vegetables must be near the top of the oven. Using a pre-heated oven at 200°C (400°F) Mark 6, whole beetroot will take between 1½ and 2 hours, large potatoes 1 to 1½ hours, and root vegetables chopped into medium sized chunks 45 minutes to an hour. They need to be checked frequently to avoid scorching.

The vegetables should be placed with a little oil in a baking dish or tray and they should not be over-crowded

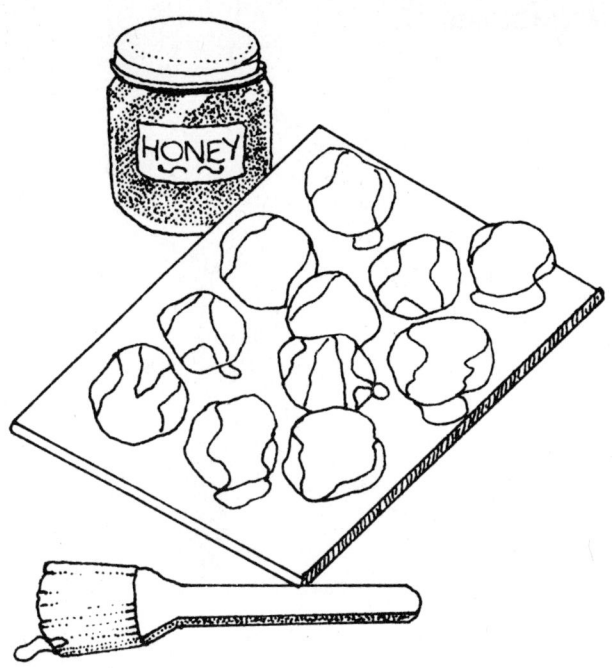

or the cooking time will be longer. If the outside of the vegetable starts to scorch before the centre is tender, save the situation by continuing the cooking on a lower heat under a sheet of foil.

Jacket potatoes

Pre-heat the oven to 200°C (400°F) Mark 6. Take 2 medium good quality potatoes per person and scrub them, remove any green patches or blemishes, and prick the skins all over with a fork. Put them on a high shelf and bake for 45 minutes. Check by inserting a fork and if the centre is tender, they are ready. Large potatoes will take longer, and small potatoes will simply evaporate, leaving a dry, empty skin. Keep to potatoes all the same size for even cooking. Serve with butter, salt, black pepper and grated cheese, cottage cheese or salted yoghurt.

Glazed roast pumpkin

3lb pumpkin for 6 people (it loses weight due to evaporation)
salt, black pepper and nutmeg or ginger to taste
1 tbsp honey (liquid)
1 tbsp vegetable oil

Peel pumpkin, remove seeds, and chop into large cubes. Stir the salt, pepper and nutmeg or ginger into the honey and using a pastry brush coat the pumpkin with the spiced honey. Oil a baking dish and put in the pumpkin and place in a pre-heated oven at 200°C (400°F) Mark 6. Bake for 30 minutes, then check with a fork that it is tender. It should be golden brown.

Cooked vegetables

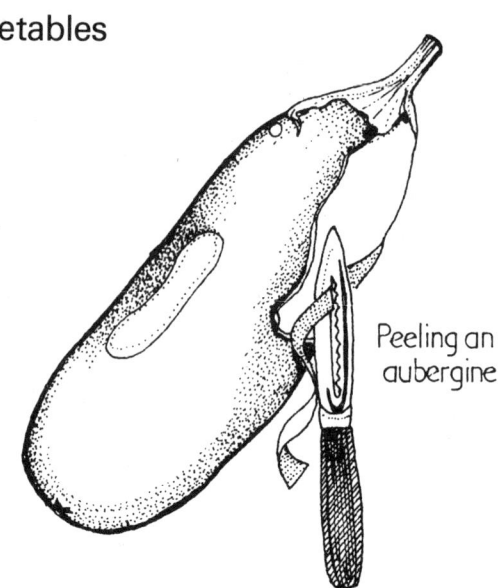

Peeling an aubergine

Mixed vegetables

A good accompaniment for a lentil pie or bean casserole. Scrub and chop a selection of winter vegetables to fit your appetites. Carrots, parsnips and swedes are excellent because they make a colourful display but potatoes and small whole onions are old favourites too. Pre-heat the oven to 200°C (400°F) Mark 6, oil a baking tray and arrange the vegetables in the tray. Dust them with salt and pepper and brush on just a little more oil. Cover with foil and bake for 20 minutes, then remove foil and bake 20 minutes more before testing with a fork. They may need a little longer.

Baked red cabbage

1 small head red cabbage, finely shredded
1 large onion, sliced in rings
2 large cooking apples, peeled, cored, and sliced

a little vegetable oil
1 cup water
salt and black pepper to taste
1 tbsp honey or molasses
1 heaped tbsp crushed caraway seeds

Pre-heat the oven to 220°C (425°F) Mark 7. In a casserole arrange layers of red cabbage, onion and apple. Sprinkle in seasonings, as you go and trickle honey or molasses over layers of apple. Pour oil and water over last. Cover and leave for 45 minutes then check. The cabbage should remain crisp and the apples should not collapse.

Serve with nut roast or other favourite winter oven dishes. A little lemon juice sprinkled over at the last minute lifts the flavour, while some like a side-dish of salted yoghurt.

Baked beetroot

Small raw beetroot should be cleaned and trimmed but not peeled. Allow 2

14

per person. Put them in a pre-heated oven, 200°C (400°F) Mark 6, on an oiled baking tray and bake for 1 hour before checking with a fork. If large, they will surely need 1½ to 2 hours. Serve whole and scoop the flesh out of the tough skins when eating.

Baked aubergine

To reduce the cooking time, buy small aubergines, 2 per person. Pre-heat the oven to 220°C (425°F) Mark 7. Prick the aubergines all over with a fork and put them on an oiled baking tray. Check with a fork after 40 minutes to see if they are tender. Remove and cool, then peel and discard skins. Mash the flesh with butter, margarine or olive oil and season with salt, black pepper and ground coriander. When you want to serve, reheat in the oven or under a grill for a few minutes.

Stuffed

Whenever you have some leftover grain, it is a good opportunity to prepare stuffed vegetables; they also make a very attractive side dish when you have guests. The stuffing is prepared first, the vegetables are hollowed and cleaned and the stuffing is put in, then the vegetables are baked in the oven.

Stuffed sweet peppers

A treat, when you can find large, inexpensive sweet peppers.

1 large sweet pepper per person
a little vegetable oil
1 small onion, chopped
a little grated carrot and chopped celery
1 dsp sultanas
a tbsp cooked brown rice per person
tamari and black pepper to taste

Prepare a large pan of boiling salted water, and put in the whole peppers for 5 minutes. Drain and cool and cut a cap off the top of each. Remove the seeds and pith carefully with a spoon.

Heat the oil, fry the onion for a few minutes, then add the carrot and celery and fry 5 minutes more, then add the sultanas and cooked rice and continue frying and stirring till all is well heated. Season well with tamari and pepper. Spoon the rice filling into the peppers and replace the caps. Pre-heat the oven to 190°C (375°F) Mark 5, place the stuffed peppers in an oiled baking dish and bake for 25 to 30 minutes.

A summer variation is to stuff the uncooked peppers with rice salad and serve the whole as a cold salad dish.

For a colourful effect you can colour the rice stuffing yellow by adding 1 tsp turmeric to the oil when frying.

Stuffed baked onions

a little vegetable oil
2oz cashew nuts
black pepper and salt
2oz mushrooms
2oz sultanas
1 cup cooked millet
½ tsp sage
1 dsp tamari
1 large onion per person

Heat the oil and fry the cashew nuts with salt and pepper till golden. Add mushrooms and sultanas and fry for 3 minutes. Add cooked millet and sage and fry till the grain is golden. Add tamari at the end.

Peel the onions and steam them for 10 minutes, then carefully scoop a hole in each. Fill with millet mixture, dot with butter and bake at 220°C (425°F) Mark 7 for 30 minutes.

Cooked vegetables

Stuffed tomatoes

1 or 2 large, firm tomatoes per person
a little vegetable oil
1 small onion, finely chopped
salt and pepper to taste
2oz mushrooms
1 small green pepper
1 cup cooked buckwheat
2oz grated cheese

Cut a cap off each tomato and scoop out some of the flesh. Heat the oil and fry the onion till transparent, then add the salt, pepper, mushrooms, green pepper finely chopped, and fry a little more. Add the buckwheat and the scooped out tomato pulp and fry till golden. Spoon the mixture into the tomatoes and put the grated cheese on top. Put the tomatoes in ½ in water in an oven dish with a blob of butter on each. Bake in a hot oven at 230°C (450°F) Mark 8 for 15 minutes.

Sweet corn

A grain that behaves like a vegetable. Sweet corn is one of the starchier grains with a lower protein content than many of the 'hard' grains, but it is a very light and palatable summer food when it is in season. Here are two slightly unusual ways of using corn on the cob.

Thai-style

Two small, young ears of corn per person with the green leaves intact. Boil a large pan of salted water, put in the corn cobs, lower the heat, and simmer 20–30 minutes, depending on the size and age of your corn cobs, till tender. (Test by parting the top leaves and pricking a few kernels with a fork.) Drain and store in a sealed plastic bag. When they are needed at the picnic, unwrap them from their organic 'package' and eat salted.

Indian-style

Two ears of corn per person, remove all the green leaves and silken threads from the cobs. Prepare a small amount of salt and red chilli powder and half a lemon for each person. Dry grill the cobs under the grill, turning on all sides till they are golden. (This works well on an outdoor camp fire too.) They will cook very quickly if young. Rub lemon juice and chilli salt on each cob before eating hot.

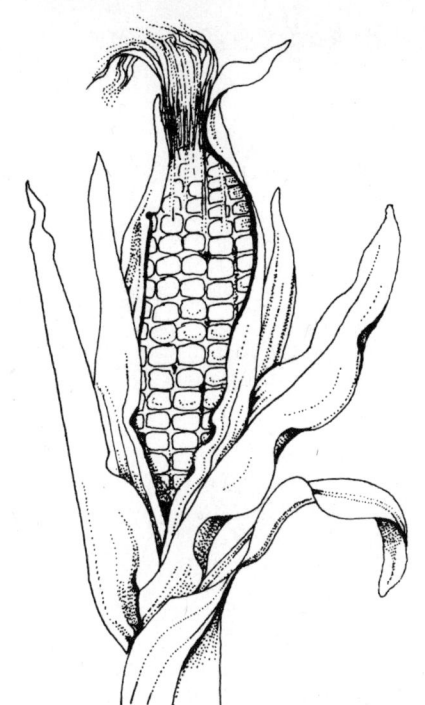

Cooked vegetables

Unusual vegetables

Lady's fingers (okra or bindi)

These unusual green vegetables, like a pointed and segmented poa pod, are available from Asian and West Indian vegetable shops and have a very unusual flavour.

1lb lady's fingers
a little vegetable oil
salt, pepper and ginger powder for seasoning
juice of 1 lemon
½ tsp garam masala

Wash and drain the lady's fingers, then heat the oil and fry them, stirring constantly. If they are small you can fry them whole but larger ones can be cut into rings or sliced in half lengthwise. Season as they cook with salt, pepper and ginger. When they are crisp, remove from heat and drain off any excess oil. Serve immediately sprinkled with lemon juice and garam masala. They taste just right with boiled rice and salted yoghurt.

Fennel

One fennel stem per person, sliced in rounds. Fennel has a texture like celery and its own unique aniseed flavour. Saute the rounds of fennel in a little butter over a gentle heat for just a few minutes and sprinkle with salt. They need no other seasoning. A fine side vegetable.

Fennel

Lady's fingers (okra)

Globe artichoke with tahini sauce

1 large or 2 small globe artichokes per person
1 mug tahini (sesame seed paste)
juice of 1 lemon
a little vegetable oil
4 cloves garlic, crushed
salt to taste

Bring a large pot of salted water to the boil. Submerge the globe artichokes in the water stem upwards and simmer for 20 minutes if small on a medium heat, 30 minutes if they are very large. Drain. Meanwhile, blend the tahini, lemon juice, vegetable oil, crushed garlic and salt to a smooth paste and put a little beside each plate in a small dish. Strip off the artichoke 'petals' and dip in tahini sauce, then eat the fleshy base of each petal, discarding the rest of the petal. When all the petals are gone, discard the 'bristles' and eat the fleshy heart, also dipped in tahini sauce.

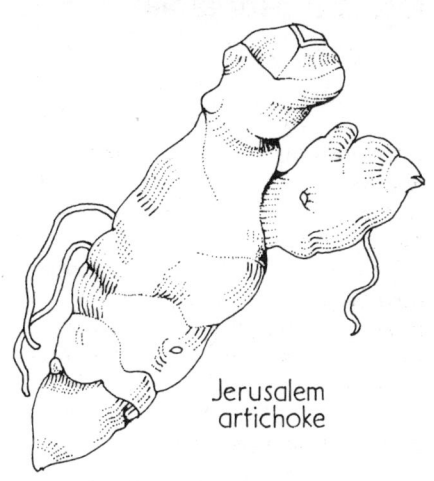

Jerusalem artichoke

Globe artichoke

Jerusalem artichoke
These nobbly little fellows should be scrubbed thoroughly, since peeling is virtually impossible. Then steam over boiling water for 7 minutes if small, 10 minutes if larger, and serve sprinkled with salt, black pepper and butter or margarine.

Kohlrabi
These are delectable little vegetables which should grow quite well in an English allotment or garden. The flavour is something between a turnip and the green stem of a cauliflower. They are best scrubbed, sliced, and steamed for 7 minutes, then eaten with butter and pepper. If you do grow your own, pick them small and tender as they go wooden and are impossible to eat if left too long.

Swiss chard
(In Australia this is called spinach — the green, leafy variety, is European.) The stems of Swiss chard are large and white like celery, and the green leaves are dark and curly. It is best to separate leaf from stem, steam the leaves and sauté the chopped stems in a little butter. A touch of lemon juice enhances the flavour.

19

Cooked vegetables

Kohlrabi

Chinese cabbage or Chinese leaves

Some of the more sensible super-markets and even the more adventurous market stall owners, now sell these regularly. But the good news is that they grow well on allotments, supplying a winter green for salads and cooking.

Stir-fried Chinese leaves

outer leaves of a Chinese cabbage, cleaned and coarsely chopped
one medium onion, chopped
½ in root ginger, peeled and grated
2 large cloves garlic, crushed
a little oil (preferably groundnut or sesame oil)
tamari (soya sauce) to taste

Heat the oil in a wok or frying pan. Fry the onion, garlic and ginger for a few seconds, then toss in the Chinese leaves. On a high heat, fry for 2 – 3 minutes, stirring constantly. Serve immediately as a side vegetable, seasoning with tamari.

Chinese leaf salad

tender inner leaves of a Chinese cabbage, cleaned and finely chopped
1 medium carrot, grated
1 rosy eating apple, grated with skin
a few sultanas
1 tbsp chopped walnuts

Toss all the ingredients in a salad bowl. Make a basic French dressing, but add a pinch of powdered ginger. At the last minute before serving, toss the salad in the dressing.
    A classy winter salad.

Sweet potato

In texture, these knobbly root vegetables are like a floury potato, but their flavour is a delicious variation. Nutritionally they are very similar to the normal potato. Nowadays they are often available in supermarkets, but in my experience they will be cheaper from an Asian greengrocer. Below are a number of ideas for cooking them, but preparation always needs care. Once you have scrubbed them clean, peel them beside a basin of cold water. As soon as they are peeled, plunge them into water or they will start to turn black. They are still percectly edible if this happens but they look less appetising.

Mashed sweet potato

Peel, cut into chunks, put into salted water and boil till tender like a potato.

(It takes about the same time.) Drain and mash with butter and white pepper.

Roasted sweet potato
Cut into large chunks, put on an oven tray, sprinkle with oil, salt and garam masala or nutmeg and bake in a pre-heated oven at 220°C (425°F) Mark 7 until golden and tender. Serve as a side vegetable.

Sweet potato crisps
So delicious it is worth eating a little fried food for once! Cut the chips very thinly, have the oil hot and they will fry crisp and gold quickly without absorbing much grease. Eat just salted — vinegar would be quite superfluous.

Yam
Another tuber similar to a sweet potato. There are several varieties. The one I like and trust is smaller than most with a skin like a red potato. The flesh inside is orange. When oven-baked in its skin then peeled it has a more moist flesh than potatoes. Salt and a pinch of ginger enhances the flavour.

Daikon (Japanese radish)
A large vegetable like a white carrot which should be chopped and steamed, then eaten with tamari (soya sauce).

Choko
Another tropical vegetable familiar to West Indians, Indians and Australians. Choko is the colour of an eating apple, shaped rather like a pear and it is like a firm-fleshed marrow, but holds its texture and flavour so much better than marrow when cooked. Peel, cut out the seed at the centre, and slice, then either steam or sauté in a little butter. Sprinkle on a little ginger, coriander or nutmeg as a change from the usual pepper.

Dandelion root
In autumn, if you are near a field or patch of waste ground where the weeds have been undisturbed for 2 to 3 years, you can dig up the roots of dandelions — you will be surprised how large they are. Scrub them, slice in rounds, and stir-fry in a little vegetable oil, then serve sprinkled with tamari.

Some of the vegetables above might seem a bit whimsical, but they are all delicious, and there is no reason why health food has to be a joyless afair — dabbling with exotic and unfamiliar vegetables certainly helps to make your diet more enjoyable.

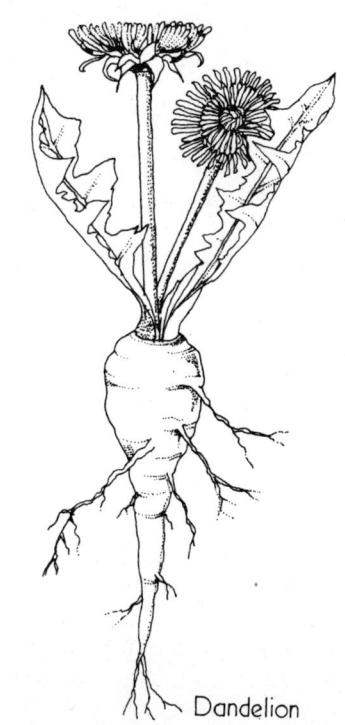

Dandelion

Cooked vegetables

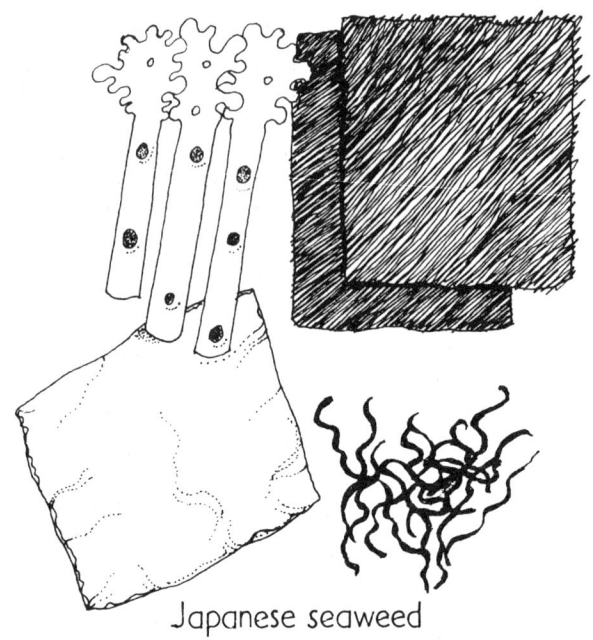

Japanese seaweed

Sea vegetables

These are a very good source of minerals in the diet. Their smell when uncooked and their appearance can be alarming – not a good dish to serve to a timid friend you are hoping to convert to health food cookery! But they are worth experimenting with, as you will find them tasty and easy to use.

Nori

This seaweed is dried on frames into tissue-thin sheets which are almost black. You should toast each sheet over a naked flame for a few minutes till it turns green and becomes crumbly. (It is fun to do it over a candle at the table.) Then crumble the nori over soup, or rice and vegetables as a savoury garnish.

Kombu

This comes in crumbled, dried strips. When washed and soaked they open out like a large liquorice strap. One strip of washed kombu simmered in a pint of water for 5 minutes makes a useful stock for soups, stews or casseroles. Alternatively you could immerse the kombu strip in your stew and discard it at the end of cooking.

Wakame (Dulse)

This also comes in large, flat strips like liquorice straps. If soaked overnight and then simmered for 30 minutes, it can be served like a green vegetable, sprinkled with tamari.

Dulse and carrots

I hope you can develop a liking for dulse with its sinister science fiction texture and dark purple colour. It is plentiful around the British coast and is especially useful in winter when the range of nutritious vegetables gets narrower. Here it is used in a substantial winter side dish, excellent with a main course of grains and pulses.

½ pkt dried dulse, soaked overnight
1 medium onion
1 small carrot per person
1 tbsp toasted sesame seeds
a little oil
sea salt

Chop the onion coarsely. Drain the dulse and heat the oil. Fry the onion 2 minutes, then add the dulse and stir into the hot oil. Add 2 tbsp water, lower the heat, cover and simmer for 20 minutes. (Check it does not dry out.)

Clean the carrots, chop into slim strips, and put into a steamer. Cook 5 – 7 minutes till crisp but tender. Arrange on a bed of dulse in a serving dish, sprinkle with sesame seeds and season lightly with sea salt.

Hizike

Hizike comes in the form of almost black curly threads. If soaked overnight and then steamed or gently simmered for 30 minutes it can be served with rice and vegetables. It also complements the flavours of both aduki and soya beans.

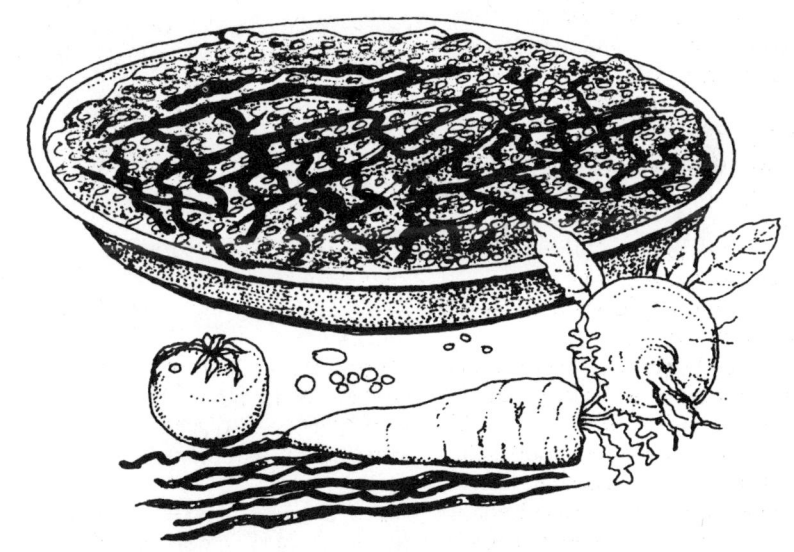

Vegetable-based soups

In these days of tins and packets soup making is perhaps a dying art. Maybe it is the image of pots simmering for hours that puts people off. The possibility of tasty soups made entirely from vegetables and a few herbs seems to surprise a lot of my friends, especially when they discover that the soups can be made quickly. Some are substantial enough to make a main meal, with the right accompaniments.

Stock pot

A lot of flavour and food value goes into the dustbin which could be used in the form of vegetable stock. Whenever you are preparing vegetables, set aside the peelings, coarse greens, stems and tops and also things like pea pods which you would normally discard. Wash them thoroughly and discard any blighted bits, then simmer on a very gentle heat in a good quantity of water. You can leave the stock pot simmering as long as you are in the kitchen. When a good stock forms, strain, cool and discard the vegetable pieces and store the stock in a clean jar in the fridge till needed. It is best to use it within 3 days so that its food value does not deteriorate. You can flavour your stock with a few herbs or spices and salt, but it is more versatile if you do not and it can be used in any soup, stew, curry, or casserole. Cooking water from pulses is another nourishing and flavoursome form of stock.

Clear Brown Soups (using miso and tamari)

Miso is a very valuable vegetable product made from fermented soya beans. It forms a dark brown paste, and just 1 dsp will make sufficient stock for soup for 4. Rather than adding salt, try seasoning it with **tamari**, the best form of soya sauce available, since it has no artificial preservatives. When using these 2 products, always add them at the end of cooking and do not boil, since this destroys the natural enzymes which are an important part of their nutritional value.

Basic clear miso soup

1 tbsp oil
2pts hot water
1 tbsp miso
1 dsp tamari

Heat the oil. Put in most of the hot water and bring to the boil. Dissolve the miso and tamari in the remaining hot water. Take off the heat and stir the miso mixture into the water. Serve at once.

Miso vegetable soup (a Chinese style consommé)

Begin by preparing 2pts basic clear miso soup.

For a richer flavour: select either 1 tsp chilli or 1in piece of root ginger, or a small clove of crushed garlic and fry into the oil before making the miso stock.

For a sweet and sour soup: add the juice of 1 lemon and 1 tbsp of apple or pineapple juice, 1 tbsp honey and 1 tbsp wine or cider vinegar.

Select 1½lb weight of available crisp vegetables, from the following list: celery, carrot, white cabbage, spinach, sweet pepper, radish, daikon, aubergine, mushroom, green peas or green beans. Onion or spring onion is essential.

Clean the vegetables and chop them finely or grate them, salt lightly and sauté in a little oil until cooked but crisp. Add them to the miso soup as soon as it is cooked and serve at once. Seaweeds such as wakame and hizike can be prepared beforehand and added to this soup. If you can find it, soya bean curd (tofu) cut into small cubes and sautéed, is a superb addition.

This soup is very good accompanied by croutons, chopped cress, parsley or coriander, pickled umeboshi plums, poached egg, or nori, a paper thin toasted seaweed.

Thick miso soup

A useful quick meal if you have some left-over cooked rice or beans.

1½lbs chopped crisp vegetables salted and sautéed
1 mug cooked brown rice
1 mug cooked soya, aduki or other beans
2pts clear miso soup

When the vegetables are thoroughly cooked, add the rice and beans, which must be thoroughly drained beforehand, and continue stirring till all is well heated. Then prepare the basic miso soup, and add the cooked vegetables, grains and beans just before serving. Best accompaniments are hizike seaweed or thick buttered brown bread.

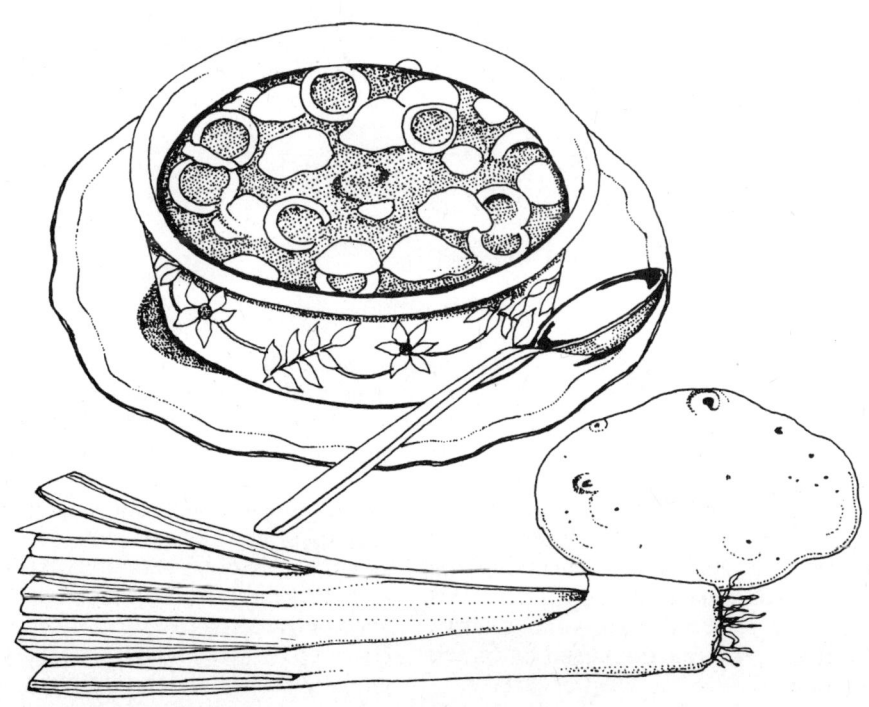

Vegetable-based soups

French onion soup

a little butter or oil
1lb Spanish onions, finely chopped
1 dsp sesame seeds
1 tbsp bread crumbs
2pts water or stock
2 dsp miso
3 tsp tamari
1 tsp each sage, tarragon and rosemary

Heat the butter or oil and fry the onions till tender and transparent. Add sesame seeds and breadcrumbs and fry for 5 minutes more. Add the stock or water and herbs, bring to the boil, lower heat and simmer for 7 minutes. Add miso and tamari and stir well. Serve, accompanied by croutons, cracker biscuits or grated cheese.

Brown leek and potato soup

1lb potatoes, scrubbed and cut in rounds
1lb leeks, well cleaned and chopped
2 cloves garlic, crushed
1 tsp ginger, 1 tsp oregano
1 tbsp butter
2pts water or stock
2 dsp miso
3 tsp tamari

Fry the potato, leek and garlic with the ginger and oregano in the butter until the leeks are transparent. Add stock or water and simmer till the potatoes are tender. Add miso and tamari, stir well and serve immediately, accompanied by brown bread and butter, toast or cheese.

Tomato based soups

Some health food cooks shun tomatoes since they are of the same plant family as deadly nightshade, but Western medicine values them highly as a source of vitamin C (ascorbic acid). Their food value is highest when they are eaten raw as a salad, preferably chopped just before eating. As a soup base they are colourful, sweetly flavoured and quickly cooked, but not high in food value. Remember that tomatoes are acidic, so a meal starting with tomato soup should not feature vinegar, lemon or other acidic food in later courses.

Basic tomato soup

oil or butter for frying
1 large onion, finely chopped
2 cloves crushed garlic
2lb chopped ripe tomatoes
salt and black pepper to taste
1pt liquid (water, milk or half milk and half water)
large pinch ginger
1 tsp basil
1 tsp thyme
1 dsp honey or brown sugar
1 dsp tamari

Heat the oil and fry the onions and garlic till tender and transparent. Add tomatoes, salt and pepper. Lower the heat and simmer till pulpy, then mash. Stir in 1pt liquid and remaining seasonings, heat but do not boil, and simmer for 20 minutes. If using milk, keep the heat low or the acid of the tomatoes will cause the milk to separate. Good accompaniments include yoghurt, sour cream, lemon juice, crumbled crackers, croutons, chopped greens, toast, or simply whole wheat bread and butter.

Tomato noodle soup

The above soup could be built up to something more substantial by the addition of 3oz of Chinese noodles. Put the uncooked noodles into the soup after the liquid has been added, and simmer until the noodles are quite tender.

Meatless minestrone

All the ingredients as for 1pt of basic tomato soup (ie half)
1½lb chopped raw vegetables such as carrots, onions, celery, cabbage, green peppers, mushrooms and aubergines
1 cup vermicelli or other fine noodles

Begin preparing the basic tomato soup and once you have mashed the tomatoes and added the liquid, add the vegetables and simmer gently for 30 minutes. After 10 minutes, prepare the noodles or other pasta in salted water and cook for 15 minutes. Drain, and add to the soup for the last 10 minutes. Accompaniments are either Parmesan cheese or thick buttered bread.

Vegetable-based soups

Creamy soups

All these soups use the following basic technique: cook the vegetables with their seasonings till tender, then mash to a purée. Combine this with a thin, basic white sauce, adjust the seasonings, then cook gently a little longer till the flavours blend.

Accompany with whole wheat bread and butter, croutons or toast.

Basic white sauce stock

2oz butter or oil
2oz flour (whole wheat)
1pt milk (vegans could use water)
salt to taste

Melt the butter in the soup pan on a gentle flame. Add the flour gradually, stirring constantly with a wooden spoon and continue to cook till the flour absorbs the butter or oil. Add the milk gradually, stirring continuously to avoid lumps. When milk is simmering below boiling point, season with salt. The sauce is now ready to combine with any of the vegetables suggested in the recipes below.

Cauliflower cheesy soup

1 onion, chopped
1 head cauliflower, divided into small florets
1pt basic white sauce stock
½ tsp white pepper
2 tsp tamari
1 tsp nutmeg
2oz grated hard cheese

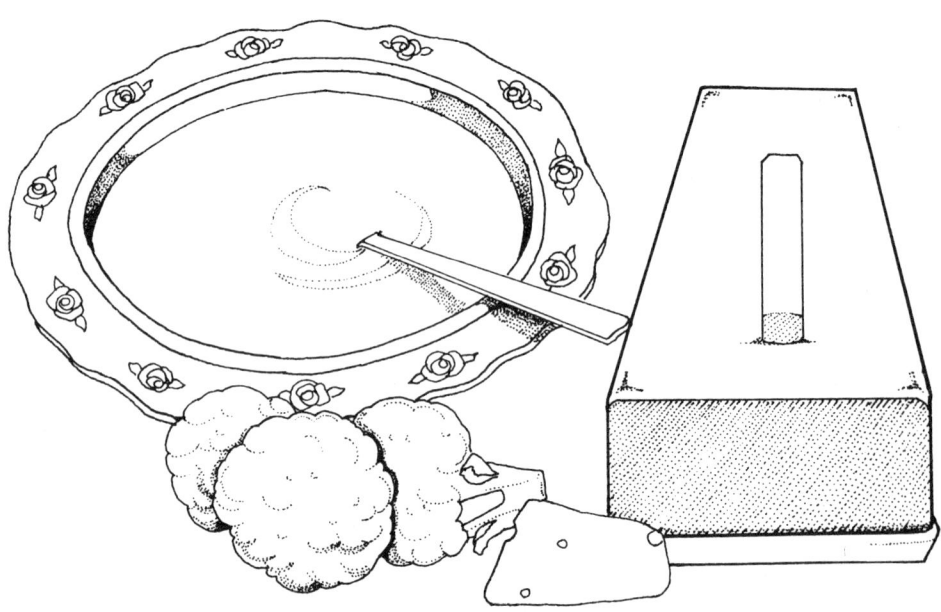

Cook the onion and cauliflower for 5 to 10 minutes in a little hot, salted water. Drain off cooking water and set it aside. Mash the cauliflower and onion to a smooth purée.

Place the white sauce on a gentle flame, add pepper, tamari and nutmeg and stir well. Add the cauliflower purée and simmer for 5 minutes, stirring continuously. Add grated cheese and cook till it melts completely. If your soup needs more liquid, stir in a little of the vegetable cooking water. If this water is not needed, put it into your vegetable stock pot. Good with buttered bread.

Cream dream soup

2lb potatoes, chopped
1 onion, chopped
1pt white stock
½ tsp black pepper
pinch ginger
1 dsp sesame seeds
1 small clove garlic
1 tbsp chopped parsley
1 dsp tamari

Cook the potatoes and onion in lightly salted water till tender, then drain and mash. Reserve the cooking water in case your soup needs more liquid. Simmer the white stock gently and season with pepper and ginger. Roast the sesame seeds and garlic in a pan with a smear of oil till crisp and golden. Add to sauce. Stir in potato purée, parsley and tamari, and simmer gently for 10 minutes. If more liquid is needed, add a little vegetable cooking water. Best accompaniment is whole wheat bread and butter.

Mushroom soup

1lb good mushrooms, chopped
1 onion, chopped
a little butter or oil
½ tsp ginger
½ tsp black pepper
1 tsp mixed herbs
tamari to taste
1½pts white sauce stock

Fry the mushrooms and onions gently in a little butter or oil. Season with ginger, pepper and herbs and, when just cooked, the tamari. Pour into the white sauce and stir well, and continue to simmer gently for a further 5 minutes. If the soup is too thick, blend in a little hot water, stir, test seasonings, and simmer for a further 5 minutes. Best accompaniments are croutons or whole wheat toast.

Pumpkin soup

2oz butter or oil
1 large onion, chopped
2lb pumpkin, peeled and cubed
salt and pepper to taste
1 tsp cummin
1 tsp ginger
1pt white sauce stock
1 bunch cress, parsley or coriander greens, chopped
tamari to taste

Heat the butter or oil and fry onion till transparent, then add pumpkin. Season with salt, pepper, cummin and ginger, and stir. Cover and simmer gently for 15 minutes. Mash the pumpkin. Add the white sauce stock, and return to a gentle heat. Add greens and tamari just before you serve. Accompaniments are grated cheese or buttered whole wheat bread.

(Marrow or courgette can be substituted for pumpkin for a more delicately flavoured soup. Do not peel them or remove the seeds.)

Vegetable-based soups

Cream of celery soup

a little oil
1 onion, chopped
1 clove garlic
1 large potato, chopped
1 small bunch celery, chopped
½ tsp white pepper
tamari to taste
1 tsp ground coriander seed
1 tsp thyme
1½ pts white sauce stock

Heat the oil, fry the onion and garlic till transparent, add the potato, celery and seasonings and fry for a further 5 minutes. Add ½ cup of water and simmer gently till tender. Mash or blend. Now combine with white sauce, using the cooking juices from the vegetables. Cook gently for 10 minutes. Good with brown bread and butter.

Pure vegetable soups

Winter vegetable soup

a little oil
1 large onion, chopped
2 cloves garlic, crushed
2lb chopped root vegetables: carrot, swede, turnip, parsnip, potato
salt and black pepper to taste
1 bay leaf or 3 juniper berries
1 tsp each rosemary and sage
1½ pts water or vegetable stock

oats or wholewheat flour to thicken
tamari to taste

Heat the oil in the pan, fry the onion
and garlic, and add the chopped
salted vegetables and fry for 10
minutes. Add pepper and herbs and
the stock or water and bring to the
boil, then lower the heat to simmer.
Gradually add 1 tbsp of flour or oats,
stirring to prevent lumps, then cover
and simmer for 1 hour. Add a little
tamari before serving with buttered
whole wheat bread. (Plain porridge
oats in small quantities are excellent
to thicken soups and stews; they give
a creamy, lump-free texture.

Debbie's 'Soup of the Gods'

1 large onion, sliced
2 cloves garlic, crushed
water and cooking oil
1 large carrot, chopped
1 large potato, chopped
any other chopped vegetables in
small quantities
mixed herbs of your choice
1pt milk
salt, pepper, tamari to taste

Fry the onion and garlic in oil in your
soup pan for a few minutes, then add
the vegetables and continue to fry
gently. Add enough water to cover,
plus the herbs, and cook for 20
minutes, or till tender. Remove the
vegetables from their juices, but
reserve these. Mash or blend the
vegetables and return them to their
juices. Add milk and reheat. Add a
little tamari and serve with bread.

Green jade soup

oil or butter for frying
1 large onion, chopped
2 cloves garlic
salt and black pepper to taste

1 tsp ginger
1 tsp coriander
2lb spinach, washed and shredded
½ cup oats
1½pts milk, water or stock
tamari to taste

In the soup pan, fry the onion, garlic
and all seasonings except the tamari
till onions are tender. Stir in spinach
and sauté gently for 7 minutes. Pour
over the liquid and bring to the boil,
then immediately lower the heat.
Carefully stir in the oats and simmer
for 15 minutes. Add tamari just
before serving. If milk is not used a
dash of lemon juice enlivens the
flavour. Serve with croutons or toast.

Red dragon soup

1½lb small raw beetroots, whole and
scrubbed
1½pts vegetable stock
1 sliced onion
2 cloves garlic, crushed
1 tsp rosemary
1 tsp ginger
salt and black pepper to taste
½pt yoghurt
1 dsp tamari

Place beetroot and stock in pot, bring
to boil, lower heat and simmer briskly
for 2 to 3 hours with the lid on till
tender. (You could substitute cooked
beetroot and begin the recipe here.)
   Fry the onion, garlic, herbs and
spices till onion is soft and
transparent, then pour contents of
the frying pan over the cooked
beetroot. Cook for 30 minutes more
on a high heat. Remove beetroot
from the pot and chop, then return it
to the soup. Season with tamari and
put a large spoon of yoghurt in the
centre of each bowl of soup. (This is
vegetarian borscht.) Chopped greens
are an attractive accompaniment.

Vegetable-based soups

Chinese jade flower soup

1½lb dried peas soaked overnight and cooked 1½ hours (or 1lb, shelled weight, fresh peas)
seasonings for dried peas: 1 bay leaf, salt and pepper to taste, 1 dsp honey and 1 tsp fresh chopped mint
1½pts basic white sauce
Seasonings for fresh peas: omit the bay leaf and pepper

If using dried peas, place the soaked peas, well covered with water, with the seasonings in a heavy pan, bring to the boil, lower heat and cook for 1½ hours, till quite tender, then mash to a purée. With fresh peas, cook with seasonings for about 20 minutes till tender then mash to a purée.

Prepare 1½pts of basic white sauce, setting aside ½pt. Combine pea purée with 1pt white sauce and simmer for 10 minutes. Keep the additional ½pt hot. Serve in bowls with a spoonful of white sauce in the centre of each, so that a white 'lotus flower' floats in the jade green soup.

Cucumber soup

1 large cucumber
1½pts yoghurt
½pt milk or water
salt and black pepper to taste
1 dsp chopped fresh mint or chives
1 small onion, finely chopped
a little paprika

Finely chop the cucumber, leaving the skin intact so that strands of white and green are pleasantly blended. Mix yoghurt with milk or water, beat in salt, pepper and the herb of your choice. Mix in the cucumber and onion. Chill. Just before serving, sprinkle a little paprika on each bowl of soup. (This Middle European summer soup is akin to the Asian side dish raita.)

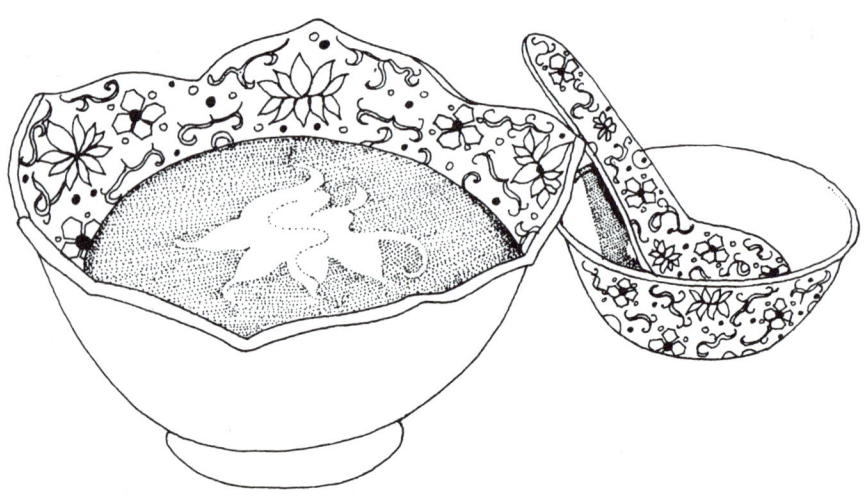

Peanut soup

Peanuts are not nuts, you know — they are vegetables; root nodules to be exact. If you like their distinctive flavour, proceed gleefully with this uncommon recipe.

½ lb dark, chunky peanut butter
1 heaped tbsp raw peanuts, chopped
1 medium onion, finely minced
3 cloves garlic, crushed
a little groundnut or other good oil
1 heaped black pepper and chilli
tamari to taste
cress or parsley to garnish
1pt warm water

Heat the oil gently and fry the onion, garlic and chopped peanuts for 5 minutes. Add the flour to form a roux. Build up a smooth soup by gradually stirring in the warm water over a gentle heat. Season with chilli and pepper, and simmer for 10 minutes. Stir in the peanut butter and continue cooking till well-blended. Season to taste with tamari just before serving. Garnish with greens.

Like me, you may like the earthy texture with chunks of peanut. If you don't, smooth it out in a blender.

A little coconut milk makes the soup even better when available.

Salads

Pulses
General information

The arguments in favour of cutting down the amount of meat in the 'average' English diet seem to be growing every day. You do not have to be a 'health food crank' to realize that too much animal fat is a major cause of obesity and heart disease. In any case, meat is more expensive week by week so that many families on a modest income have to fall back on the cheaper cuts which are not such good sources of protein. When we consider factory farming methods, the cruelty repels some of us, and certainly the unnatural chemical feeds and steroid injections and other ways by which the 'product' is 'manufactured' make meat a suspect source of wholefood.

You may be influenced by one or all of these considerations. But if you want to prepare at least some meatless meals, you do not want the nutritional balance in your diet to suffer. All the dried beans and lentils which we call 'pulses' are useful for keeping up your protein intake.

Many cooks new to health food approach pulses very timidly. There is a fear that the cooking process is long and fiddly, that they are hard to digest, that they will taste like butter beans in school dinners, and worst of all, that they are unfashionably cheap food!

If you always soak your pulses overnight before cooking, and cook them in a pressure cooker if you possess one, they will not take long to cook. However, it is difficult to give exact cooking times for pulses, because you cannot be certain of their age. If they have been stored too long they will be dry and tough and need longer cooking. It is fatal to try to tell yourself they will do, because if they are chewy and indigestible you will not enjoy the meal. It is, therefore, unwise to leave the cooking of dried pulses to the last minute. I usually pre-cook mine on the morning after they have been soaked. By the time we have had breakfast and washed up, they are well on the way to being tender. This might seem a bit of a bother at first reading, but it is no more difficult than defrosting food from the freezer. It soon becomes second nature. The recipes below for salads using pulses will, I hope, go some way to settling the question of whether or not they taste boring. If you are status conscious about being caught with your lentils showing, do not serve them when the Duchess comes to dinner, but the rest of the time they are a sensible economy!

I find salads a more interesting way to serve pulses than just having them as side vegetables. Beans and lentils which I find useful in salads are: butter beans, black eye beans, chick peas, whole khaki lentils (called variously green or brown), any of the kidney beans and moong beans in the form of beansprouts. With the exception of the beansprouts they must all be soaked overnight, then cooked in plenty of salted water till tender, drained and allowed to cool. Below is a table of cooking times, which assumes that the pulses are from the current year's crop. You really have no way of being sure about this unless your shopkeeper knows the date of the shipment. So allow more time in case they need to cook longer. Keep your eye on them throughout in they drink all their liquid. If you are using a pressure cooker allow just under half the time.

Cooking times for pre-soaked pulses

Black eyes	40 minutes
Butter beans	1 to 1¼ hours
Chick peas	up to 1½ hours
Khaki lentils	30 minutes
Kidney beans	45 minutes to 1 hour

Beansprouts

Some supermarkets and even some high class greengrocers now sell beansprouts by the pound, so if you are unfamiliar with them it would be simpler to buy the sprouts. But if you enjoy pottering about with things that grow it is cheaper to grow your own.

If you wish to grow beansprouts here is a simple method. To grow one pound of sprouts you would need 3 to 4oz of moong beans (dry weight). You will see special 'growing kits' in the shops of seeds of guaranteed high quality. These are excellent, but far more expensive than the ordinary moong beans for eating. So if the beans you buy seem to be in good condition, they should work perfectly well and cost much less!

Wash the sprouts well in tepid (not hot) water, then leave to soak overnight in at least twice their volume of water. Next day, transfer them to a large sweet jar after you have drained them of almost all their moisture and picked out any damaged seeds. (These will not grow and would tend to mould or ferment.) Cover the neck of the jar with a piece of muslin secured with a rubber band, so they can breathe but be dust free. Turn the jar on its side and store in a warm, dark cupboard.

Each day, take the sprouts out morning and (preferably) evening and wash them gently. Handle them as little as possible because if you break the tails they will grow no further. But as they slough off their green skins many of these will float to the top of the washing water and can be thrown away. It is not essential to pick out every single green skin as there is no harm in eating them, but it does improve the appearance of the sprouts to get rid of them.

In summer they may well grow after 4 days in the jar, but in cold weather they need longer as their growth rate slows. I had one batch in the bitter winter of 1978–9 that required 10 days. If they are healthy they can increase 4 to 6 times in volume, so if the jar starts to get crowded, move some to a new home. Danger signs are either a mouldy smell or brown patches on the beans or green shoots. If a mouldy smell starts or brown patches appear, wash well and cook at once. Green shoots mean they have gone too long and germination has proceeded beyond the initial stage. Again, the solution is to wash and eat them at once as if they are left any longer, they will taste bitter.

You can see that growing bean sprouts is only for those who enjoy watching things grow. Perhaps your children might take on the job. But you cannot really leave them unattended while you go away for a weekend. Not very good for forgetful people either!

Salads

Common salad vegetables are expensive for the greater part of the year and the nutritional importance of salads is often not understood. We eat raw fruits and vegetables, as fresh as possible, to get the full nutritional benefit of the foods, undamaged by any cooking process. Raw foods also stimulate our digestion and cleanse our bodies.

If your vision of a salad is one wilted lettuce leaf with some dried-up rounds of tomato, beetroot and cucumber, you will shudder at the idea of eating salads often. But expand your vision to take in all kinds of vegetables raw, many fruits, nuts, dried fruits, grains and beans, as well as eggs and cheese and you can see it might be fun as well as healthy.

Salads make good summer main meals, but try to eat 2 or 3 side salads each week in winter also for good health.

Dressings

French dressings and variations

2 parts good vegetable oil (soya, sunflower or corn)
1 part lemon juice, or wine or cider vinegar
salt and freshly ground black pepper to taste
a little honey (optional)

In summer you can make a fairly big batch and store it in the fridge in a non-metallic container. Shake before using.

This basic dressing can be varied in the following ways.
Orange, lime, grapefuit or apple juice instead of lemon juice.
Olive oil for a Mediterranean flavour.
Garlic or mustard gives a kick for grains or beans which are bland
Your favourite herbs, fresh or dried. You can store dressing with herbs so that the flavours mature.
Coriander adds aroma and flavour.

Yoghurt dressing and variations

Take 1pt plain yoghurt and beat in a little milk till it reaches a smooth pouring consistency, then season with salt and pepper.

The following are pleasant ways of varying this dressing.

Dill seed gives an East European flavour and helps the digestion.
Chives or spring onions for a savoury tang.
Crushed garlic.
Paprika sprinkled on top for colour.
Cool green herbs such as parsley, water cress, coriander or mint.
Chopped green chilli.

Tahini dressing

½ cup tahini (sesame seed paste)
juice of 1 lemon
1 clove garlic, crushed
salt and pepper
½ tsp honey or brown sugar
a little water

Blend all the ingredients to a smooth liquid.

Salads

'Chinese' dressing

pinch ginger
1 clove garlic
½ red or green chilli
2 tbsp white vinegar or lemon juice
2 tbsp good vegetable oil
2 tsp tamari
1 tsp honey or brown sugar
salt to taste

Grind the ginger, garlic and chilli in a pestle and mortar. Add the other ingredients and beat well. Pour over any crisp salad about half an hour before serving. This makes ½ cup, sufficient for a large bowl of salad. It is a pungent dressing so you can omit the ginger or chilli if you wish.

Vegetable salads

If your salad is a colourful blend of crisp vegetables, each with a lively flavour, there is really no need for a dressing – just let yourself get to know the true flavours of your food.

Classic green salad

Ring the changes on this one: one head of the lettuce of your choice, or experiment with chicory, Chinese leaves, or endive (spiky French lettuce) if you see they are cheap. Dressing: basic French dressing with the addition of 2 cloves of crushed garlic and ½ tsp mustard powder.

Divide the green vegetable into separate leaves, wash under cold water and shake thoroughly dry. If the leaves are large, tear them coarsely with your fingers. Arrange in a bowl and pour over the dressing. Serve with a good bread as a side

dish in summer meals, with cold savoury pies, omelettes or flans. Eat as soon as possible as the acid of the dressing will quickly cause the leaves to wilt, and in any case the food value of lettuce deteriorates from the moment it is picked.

Tamatar jeera (Indian tomato salad)

1 small bunch coriander greens
1 small onion
1lb tomatoes
Dressing: basic French dressing with ½ tsp cummin added. Use lemon, or better still lime, rather than vinegar

Finely chop the coriander greens and the onion, coarsely chop the tomatoes. Gently stir them together in the salad bowl and pour over the dressing. Tomatoes start to lose food value from the moment they are picked, so eat them as soon as possible.

Green bean and tomato salad

1 small onion
8oz firm tomatoes
8oz cooked green beans, drained and cold
Dressing: basic French dressing with 1 tsp coriander added

Finely chop the onion and coarsely chop the tomato. Mix with the cold beans and pour the dressing over the salad. Serve immediately.

Nitza's aubergine salad
Aubergines also are perishable so you can sometimes find them in good condition but being sold cheap before a holiday or weekend. A few blemishes do no harm in this recipe as they can be cut out.

3 good sized aubergines
½ clove garlic
1 onion
1 sweet red pepper
1 tbsp olive oil
juice of 1 lemon
salt and black pepper

Peel and slice the aubergines and then stand them in salted water for half an hour until they release some of their bitter juices. Drain well. Fry lightly with garlic and perhaps a little water if they tend to burn. When tender, remove from heat and mash. Chop the onion and red pepper finely and mix in. Beat the olive oil with lemon juice, salt and pepper and add.

Good with rice, Greek bread (pitta), yoghurt, cream cheese, corn on the cob, other salads or cold summer flans.

Avocado salad
Avocados are perishable fruits, so you may occasionally see a stall or shop selling them cheap before weekend closing. Then you can buy a good batch and enjoy this treat.

1 tbsp oil (preferably olive)
juice of ½ a lemon
salt and black pepper to taste
½ tsp freshly ground coriander
1 small onion
1 small sweet red pepper
3 large or 6 small avocado pears

Beat the oil, lemon juice, salt, pepper and coriander, and leave to stand. Finely mince the onion and sweet red pepper. Peel the avocados, cut them in half lengthwise and remove the stones. Place all the avocado flesh in a bowl and mash well. Stir in onion and red pepper and beat in the dressing. Serve chilled. Delicious with cottage cheese and bread.

Salads

individual serving dishes with the creamy sauce poured over, and garnished with chopped cress or parsley.

Cold baked beetroot, Balkans-style

2 small beetroots per person
½pt yoghurt, or sour cream
salt and crushed dill seed to taste
(If dill is not available, caraway, cummin or fennel seeds can be substituted)
cress or parsley to garnish

Bake the beetroot in their jackets as described above in the section on baked vegetables. Make sure they are tender right through to the centre. When cool, peel, leaving them whole, and chill.

Beat the seasonings into the yoghurt or sour cream. Bring the beetroot to the table in small

Potato salad

3 spring onions or 1 small onion
1 sprig parsley
1lb potatoes
Dressing: 1 cup yoghurt dressing

Finely mince the spring onions, green parts as well as white, with the parsley. Mix onion and parsley with cold boiled potatoes, cut in large chunks. Pour over yoghurt dressing and serve at once, for potatoes tend to go black.

Coriander greens or sweet pepper could be substituted for the parsley. Cucumber, grated carrot and cold cooked green peas or beans can all be added for a bigger salad.

Sweet corn salad

1 large ear of corn per person
½ a cucumber
2 sticks celery
8oz firm tomatoes
1 medium onion
1 small red and 1 small green sweet pepper
1 small head lettuce
Dressing: either French dressing or yoghurt

Pre-cook the corn cobs by simmering for 20 to 30 minutes in salted water, then drain. When cool, remove the kernels from the cobs with a knife. Finely chop the cucumber, celery, tomatoes, onion and sweet peppers and toss with the corn kernels in a bowl. Divide the lettuce into leaves, wash and drain. Fill each lettuce leaf with corn salad and arrange the lettuce cups on a serving plate, with dressing poured over each.

Winter salad

1 small head white cabbage, shredded shredded
1 large or 2 small raw beetroots, grated
2 carrots, grated
1 onion, finely chopped
½ cup sultanas
1 large apple or orange, chopped
a handful of nuts
Dressing: either French, Yoghurt or Chinese dressing is good

Toss all the fruits and vegetables in a large bowl, and pour over the dressing of your choice, then sprinkle on the chopped nuts. This salad can be stored overnight without damage.

Winter salad requires no expensive out of season fruits or vegetables but is a good source of vitamins and minerals.

Tropical salad

1 head crisp lettuce
8oz tomatoes
3 spring onions
1 small red or green sweet pepper
2 sticks celery
½ cup pineapple cubes
1 large, unblemished banana
the juice of 1 large orange
Dressing: basic French dressing with coriander added

Wash all the salad vegetables and chop in attractive shapes. Arrange with the pineapple cubes and banana in a salad bowl. You can either toss them or make a formal arrangement. Pour over plenty of dressing and eat immediately as the ingredients are very perishable. A good complete meal with cheese, cottage cheese, cold hard boiled eggs or rice and chutney.

Jewel Mountain salad

If you have a big, compartmentalised serving dish, this salad makes a very attractive and colourful centrepiece for a summer lunch or party. (A tray with an arrangement of small bowls looks equally attractive).

Not only does it look pretty, but it is very practical – the guests can choose their ingredients, and also their dressings, so everyone is happy.

The 'jewel mountains' are piles of brightly-coloured diced or shredded salad vegetables. My favourite selection is tomato, carrot, beetroot, cucumber with skin left on, sweet corn kernels, and green peppers – but the variations are endless.

Besides the 'mountains' arrange small dishes of the following dressings – yoghurt dressing, tahini dressing, mayonnaise and simple French dressing.

Salads

Grain salads

Wild greens summer salad

If you are new to this area of food, try this out for yourself before springing it on family and friends. I suspect that if you tell some people you are eating weeds and flowers they won't even try — tell them later! Preferably when they ask for more . . .

1 small head of lettuce
a selection from the following, fresh-picked, cleaned and finely chopped: small tender dandelion leaves, nasturtium leaves, thyme, lemon balm, wild sorrel, borage, parsley, and a touch of mint

Wash, shake and tear the lettuce coarsely. Clean and finely mince the herbs and blend in with the lettuce. Chop a small onion and add this to the greens.
Dressing: Oil, lemon juice, honey and a little salt, well-blended. Pour the dressing over at the last minute to avoid wilting the greens.

Cucumber raita

salt and pepper to taste
½ cup yoghurt
1 large cucumber
generous pinch paprika
1 small bunch coriander greens or cress

Beat salt and pepper into the yoghurt and thin it a little with milk if it is very solid. (It should be like whipped cream.) Chop the cucumber in small, decorative shapes, leaving green skin intact. Stir into the yoghurt and just

Billy Michael's Lebanese cracked wheat salad

1lb cooked bulgher (cracked wheat), drained and cold
1 handful of stoned dates, minced
1 green sweet pepper, finely chopped
1 onion, finely chopped
1 cup yoghurt dressing with a little crushed garlic and coriander

Cracked wheat is easy to manage. Dry roast 8oz at a time in the bottom of a saucepan for about 1 minute till a toasted smell rises. Stir with a wooden spoon so it does not scorch while roasting! Cover with twice its volume of salted cold water and bring to the boil, then lower the heat and simmer for 20 minutes. It will absorb virtually all its own moisture so you must stir it to prevent burning for the last few minutes. Stir the dates, sweet pepper and onion into the cold, drained grain and then thoroughly blend in the yoghurt dressing.

A variation is to use tahini dressing instead of the yoghurt dressing, and this is equally delicious.

Giant brown rice salad

1 mug cooked long-grain brown rice per person
1 mug per person of chopped assorted salad vegetables (not beetroot or potato, but perhaps tomato, celery, carrot, white cabbage and raw onion)
1 red apple, chopped but not peeled
1 sweet orange divided into segments
1 dsp sultanas

1 dsp chopped roasted peanuts (or hazels if you dislike peanuts)
Dressing: ½ cup white vinegar or lemon juice
½ cup pleasant-tasting vegetable oil
a generous pinch each of salt, black pepper and ginger
1 tsp tamari

Toss all the salad ingredients thoroughly in a large salad bowl. Thoroughly beat all the dressing ingredients, then pour through the rice salad. You can see that this mammoth salad would be the centrepiece of a summer lunch or picnic.

Salads using pulses

(*see also* p 34 for a discussion of pulses and their use)

Beansprout salad

1 large apple or orange
½ cup sultanas
1 small onion
1 carrot
1lb raw beansprouts
Dressing: either French dressing with lemon juice and a pinch of ginger, or Chinese dressing. For a complete transformation use tahini dressing

Chop the apple or divide the orange in segments. Wash the sultanas, and chop the onion. Grate the carrot. Toss these in with the beansprouts and pour over the dressing of your choice.

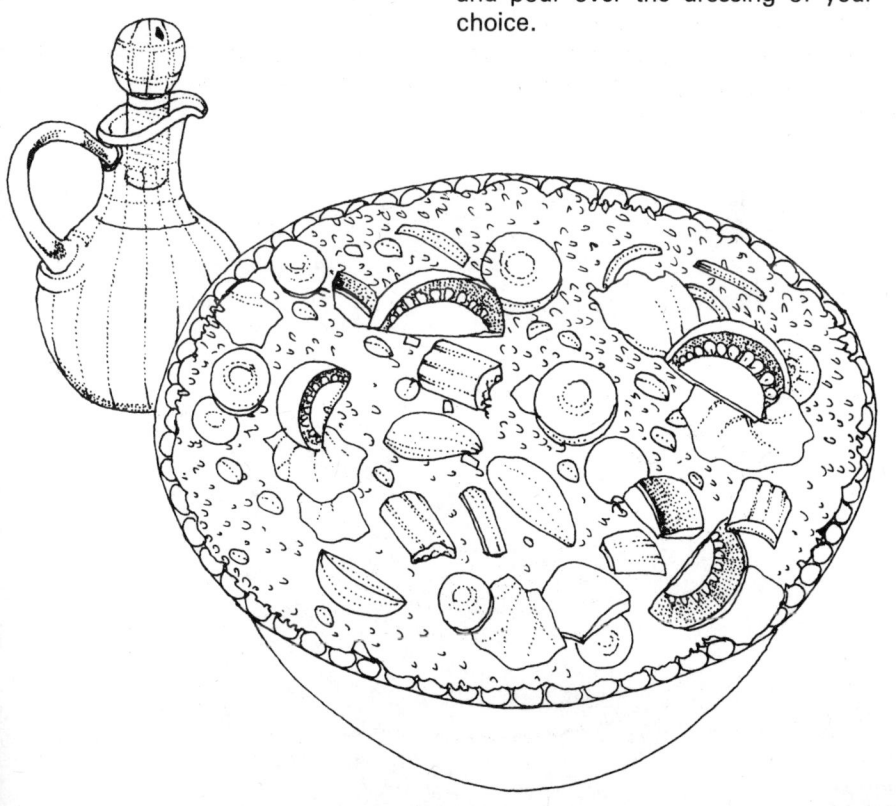

Salads

Black eye bean salad

8oz black eye beans (dry weight)
1 onion finely chopped
1 tbsp chopped cashews
1 tbsp sultanas
1 cup yoghurt and a little milk
salt to taste
1 large banana cut in rounds

This fruity salad enhances the sweet flavour of the beans. Soak the black eye beans overnight, put them in double their volume of salted water, bring to the boil, then lower the heat and simmer for approximately 40 minutes till tender. Do not let them get mushy. Drain and allow to cool.

In a salad bowl gently mix the beans with the chopped onion, cashew and sultanas. Beat up the yoghurt with a little milk till it is a smooth pouring consistency, then season with salt and mix it through the bean salad. Just before you are serving the salad, chop the banana and mix it through.

This is good served with cold rice and green salad. Substantial enough for a summer main dish.

Red bean salad

1 small onion
1 small bunch watercress or parsley
1lb cold cooked red kidney beans (cooked weight, not dry weight)
Dressing: French dressing with lemon and garlic

This is one of my favourite salads, plain as it is. If you are not using

ready-cooked beans you should start with 8oz dry weight beans, and soak them overnight before cooking.

Finely chop the onion and greens and toss with the drained, cooked beans in a bowl. Pour over the garlic French dressing and leave to stand. This makes a good centre of a summer meal with vegetable salads and cold grain.

Lentil salad

8oz dry weight khaki lentils
3 young spring onions or 1 small onion
8oz salad tomatoes
2 sticks celery
Dressing: French dressing with lemon juice and 1 tsp cummin

Cook the lentils till tender, drain and cool. Chop all the vegetables into decorative shapes and arrange with the cold lentils in a bowl. Pour over the dressing. If you really like chilli, chop one green chilli very finely and scatter it over the top of the salad, but warn any unsuspecting friends! Excellent with cold rice and yoghurt.

Spicy Egyptian lentil salad

8oz dry weight Egyptian (khaki) lentils
1 pinch chilli powder or 1 green chilli
½ clove garlic
½ tsp ground fresh root ginger
½ tsp coriander
salt and pepper to taste
1 tbsp vegetable oil
juice of ½ lemon
1 onion, finely chopped
1 sweet red pepper

Cook the lentils in plenty of salted water for 35 minutes or more till tender, but do not let them break up. Drain and cool. In a pestle and mortar grind the chilli, garlic, ginger,

coriander, salt and pepper to a paste. Beat the oil and lemon juice and stir in the spices to form a pungent dressing. Finely chop the onion and sweet pepper and mix with the drained lentils. Thoroughly stir in the spice dressing. Good with plain cold millet, buckwheat or rice.

Chick-pea salad

1 small head lettuce
3 spring onions
1 small sweet red pepper
8oz (cooked weight) cold pre-cooked chick-peas
Dressing: tahini dressing is superb, but an ordinary French dressing would be pleasant, too.

Coarsely tear the washed and drained lettuce, and finely chop the spring onions (including the green parts) and the sweet pepper. Toss these with the chick-peas and then pour over the dressing.

Butter bean salad

8oz cold, pre-cooked butter beans
1 eating apple
1 tbsp chopped dates or sultanas
Dressing: yoghurt dressing, perhaps with the herb of your choice

Stir the chopped fruits into the well-drained beans, then pour over yoghurt dressing. This can be eaten at any time of the year but I find the texture of butter beans comforting in cold weather, so it is one of my favourite winter salads.

Organizing winter salad menus

I have included a number of winter salads in this book, and I have mentioned the importance of having some fresh, uncooked foods regularly throughout the winter. Normally, we eat far too much preserved and cooked food throughout the cold months. If you eat salads regularly all winter, your whole digestive system will be stimulated, and you will get valuable vitamins, minerals, enzymes and natural sugars. I am seriously suggesting that in winter you should eat one side-salad daily and one main salad course weekly. (Probably a lunch of soup, salad and bread would be an ideal way to take the latter).

You might, if you work, have a salad lunch from the canteen or snackbar, and feel very virtuous. But those poor little wilted vegetables, so tastefully embalmed in cling-wrap, will not have a fraction of the nutritional value of salads made at home from fresh ingredients and eaten at once.

However, having made the suggestion, can I prove that it is practical? You can't really spend a large chunk of your income each winter on imported or greenhouse-grown tomatoes, lettuces, cucumbers, celery and sweet peppers. Nor are salads full of frozen peas and pickled beetroot really fulfilling our purpose. So how can you get plenty of variety, colour and flavour in winter salads at a reasonable price?

Here are a list of vegetables which are plentiful all winter, and either reasonable, or at least not astronomically priced. Use all of them in rotation for variety.

White and red cabbages
cauliflower (not cheap — occasional)
onions
carrots
mushrooms
potatoes (occasional — have to be cooked)
beetroot (stored raw — not pickled)
swedes, turnips and parsnips — can all be grated raw in small quantities if you like the flavour

To give more colour and flavour, you can add any of the following foods in small quantities: —

Fresh apples, oranges or satsumas
All kinds of nuts
Sesame or sunflower seeds
Raisins, sultanas and dates
Seaweed, cooked and drained

Varying the dressings helps winter variety also. Rotate French dressing, mayonnaise, tahini dressing, yoghurt dressing, and 'Chinese' (tamari) dressing. Vary the herbs and spices with which you flavour dressings and use the juice of citrus fruits instead of vinegar.

If your basic ingredients are inexpensive you can then buy just a little of the expensive imports occasionally, especially when you see a bargain. One medium sweet pepper will add zest to two or three large winter salads.

You can also grow sprouts — moong beans, wheat berries, alfalfa, mustard and cress can all be grown in a warm place at home. In terms of labour, it is ideal for the children in a family to do this indoor farming. Childless adults who work may prefer to grab a bag of bean sprouts from the cold counter at the super-market.

Using all these ingredients, here is a week's menu of six side salads and one main salad.

Day one
red cabbage, finely shredded
chopped apple
walnuts
lemon and oil dressing

Day two
Potato salad
chopped onion
grated carrot
sultanas
yoghurt dressing

Day three
grated raw beetroot
a little chopped onion
a few orange segments
plain French dressing

Day four
raw cauliflower florets
sliced raw mushroom
chopped onion
a little chopped sweet pepper or cress
  as available
yoghurt dressing

Day five
a little cooked seaweed (hizike or
  dulse are best) cooled, drained and
  chopped
grated carrot
a little grated turnip or parsnip —
  your choice
a *dressing* of tamari, garlic and
  ginger, diluted to taste with a little
  water

Day six
coleslaw consisting of: —
  onion, carrot and white cabbage,
  finely grated
chopped dates
sunflower seeds
tahini dressing

Day seven
Main course salad
beansprouts
chopped nuts and seeds of your
  choice
grated carrot
chopped apple
a little green vegetable for colour as
  available (e.g. cucumber with skin
  intact, cress or sweet pepper)
any dressing of your choice —
  though orange juice and oil with
  ground coriander is very fresh and
  tangy)

For a substantial salad meal, any of these ingredients and dressings can be combined with cold cooked grains such as brown rice, millet or buckwheat. Cold cooked beans are also delicious — especially chick peas, red kidney beans or butter beans. But since these ingredients are all cooked, they are not as useful as the raw salads — after all, you will be eating plenty of cooked grains and pulses in other dishes all winter.

Conversion Tables

Oven temperatures

Gas Mark ½	250°F	120°C
1	275°F	140°C
2	300°F	150°C
3	325°F	170°C
4	350°F	180°C
5	375°F	190°C
6	400°F	200°C
7	425°F	220°C
8	450°F	230°C
9	475°F	240°C

Liquid measures (approximate conversions)

1pt (20fl oz)	570ml
½pt (10fl oz)	275
¼pt (5fl oz)	150

Liquid measures (approximate conversions)

1 mug (8fl oz)	250
1 cup (6fl oz)	168
1 level tablespoon (1fl oz)	25
1 level dessertspoon (½fl oz)	12
1 level teaspoon (1/6fl oz)	5

Dry weights (approximate conversions)

1lb (16oz)	450g
½lb (8oz)	225
¼lb (4oz)	110
1oz	25
1 mug (8oz)	225
1 cup flour (5oz)	125
1 cup rice (6oz)	175
1 tablespoon (1oz)	25
1 dessertspoon (⅔oz)	18
1 teaspoon (⅓oz)	9

Thanks are due to Cranks Health Foods, and particularly to the Manager of Cranks Restaurant, Dartington, Devon, for his kind assistance with the cover photograph.

British Library Cataloguing in Publication Data
Young, Mala
  Health food cooking, vegetables and salads.
  1. Cookery (Natural foods)
  2. Cookery (Vegetables)
  3. Salads
  I. Title
  641.6'5   TX741

ISBN 0-7153-8036-2

Library of Congress Catalog Card Number: 80-68708

Text and illustrations © David & Charles Ltd, 1981
Illustrated by Susan Neale

Typeset in 10 on 11 point Univers by Typesetters (Birmingham) Ltd.
and printed in Great Britain
by Redwood Burn Ltd, Trowbridge & Esher
for David & Charles (Publishers) Limited
Brunel House Newton Abbot Devon